# Ninja Foodi Dual Zone Air Fryer Cookbook for Beginners UK

1200-Day Tasty, Easy and Healthy Recipes with British Measurements & Ingredients to Air Fry, Roast, Bake, Reheat & Dehydrate Your Favorite Meals.

Webben Ruthann

© Copyright 2022 Webben Ruthann - All Rights Reserved.

In no way is it legal to reproduce, duplicate, or transmit any part of this document by either electronic means or in printed format. Recording of this publication is strictly prohibited, and any storage of this material is not allowed unless with written permission from the publisher. All rights reserved.

The information provided herein is stated to be truthful and consistent, in that any liability, regarding inattention or otherwise, by any usage or abuse of any policies, processes, or directions contained within is the solitary and complete responsibility of the recipient reader. Under no circumstances will any legal liability or blame be held against the publisher for any reparation, damages, or monetary loss due to the information herein, either directly or indirectly.

Respective authors own all copyrights not held by the publisher.

**Legal Notice:**

This book is copyright protected. This is only for personal use. You cannot amend, distribute, sell, use, quote or paraphrase any part of the content within this book without the consent of the author or copyright owner. Legal action will be pursued if this is breached.

**Disclaimer Notice:**

Please note the information contained within this document is for educational and entertainment purposes only. Every attempt has been made to provide accurate, up-to-date and reliable, complete information. No warranties of any kind are expressed or implied. Readers acknowledge that the author is not engaging in the rendering of legal, financial, medical or professional advice.

By reading this document, the reader agrees that under no circumstances are we responsible for any losses, direct or indirect, which are incurred as a result of the use of information contained within this document, including, but not limited to, errors, omissions, or inaccuracies.

# Table of Contents

Introduction ......................................................................5

Chapter 1: Breakfast ......................................................17

Chapter 2: Vegetables ...................................................24

Chapter 3: Meats ........................................................... 31

Chapter 4: Poultry .........................................................38

Chapter 5: Appetizers and Snacks ................44

Chapter 6: Wraps and Sandwiches ................ 51

Chapter 7: Casseroles, Frittatas, and Quiches 58

Chapter 8: Desserts .......................................65

Conclusion ..................................................... 71

Appendix recipe Index ..................................72

# INTRODUCTION

Timing is the key to effective cooking, and the Ninja Foodi Dual Zone Air Fryer AF300UK makes it simple to prepare food. Its most appealing feature is its capacity to simultaneously cook two different items that may be set to be ready to eat at the same time. Should you choose, you can use the Foodi Dual Zone Air Fryer to cook two different items separately. The six-in-one appliance also allows you to max crisp, roast, reheat, dry, and bake in addition to air frying.

Looking to add a new kitchen appliance to your collection? The adaptable selection from Ninja might be right for you. The Foodi Dual Zone Air Fryer AF300UK expands Ninja's rapidly expanding line of kitchen appliances, giving us more options.

Ninja creates products to "meet the lives of busy people all over the world," and is best recognised for its line of blenders and food processors that compete with Nutribullet in terms of aesthetics and functionality. Along with blenders and food processors, the company also sells a simple-to-use selection of choppers, multi-cookers, and health grills that are all made to quickly prepare delicious cuisine.

The AF300UK, the newest addition to Ninja's lineup of specific air fryers and multi-cookers, has the most streamlined design and practical features to date. It is special in that it allows for the quick production of two different dishes. This is made possible by its Sync mode, which takes care of the hard work by making sure the food you put inside - meat in one compartment and vegetables in the other, for example - is ready at the same time.

The Ninja Foodi Dual Zone Air Fryer AF300UK has all the health advantages of a respectable air fryer because it uses little to no oil and can cook food up to 75% faster than a fan oven. Additionally, it has the capacity to perform five additional tasks, including bake for desserts when you feel like something sweet, roast for vegetables and meats, reheat for leftovers, dehydrate for veggie crisps, and max crisp for cooking frozen foods like nuggets and chips.

## Style and essential components

We have tried different air fryers, but none compare to Ninja's Foodi Dual Zone Air Fryer AF300UK. It has the capacity to cook two different items simultaneously and guarantee that they are prepared for serving together, in addition to having the ability to make healthful air-fried foods with little to no oil.

It's a very large device in terms of countertop gadgets, measuring a generous H31.5 x D35cm, yet its design is both elegant and functional. Given enough space on your worktop, its sleek black and chrome appearance makes it the kind of gadget you won't mind keeping out there.

The device is beautifully designed and ergonomic to hold. It has two separate cooking drawers that slide out effortlessly and have a 7.6 litre capacity overall. Each compartment has enough depth to cook a respectable amount of food, such as a batch of 500g sweet potato fries, a kilo of chicken, or up to 12 cupcakes. The drawer handles are easy to insert and remove and have a good grip.

When you air-fry food, a crisper plate inside each compartment aids in browning the food by allowing air to circulate around it to remove excess moisture and guarantee a crispy, golden finish. Additionally, they prevent food from clinging to the bottom of each compartment. They were straightforward to remove for hand or dishwasher cleaning, in our experience.

Along with air frying, the appliance can also max crisp, roast, reheat, dehydrate, and bake, and all of these functions are indicated on the digital control panel. It's simple for you to see how much cooking time is left in each section thanks to the countdown timer.

# Dual-Zone air fryer from ninja foodi: what you need to know

The most desirable things in life are paired. Cake and more cake, fish and chips, a jacket potato and beans, and so forth. The Dual Zone may theoretically accomplish all of this and more simultaneously. But when I put the Ninja Foodi Dual Zone Air Fryer to the test, you'll see in this review just how fantastic it is with photographs and my opinions.

The AF300UK is a sizable device. I could move it to and from my (modest) kitchen as necessary, but it wasn't easy because it weights 8.2kg. It's a really thoughtful detail that the bottom of the Air Fryer has grooves for your hands to fit into to make carrying it simpler. I would advise leaving your Ninja Foodi Dual Zone Air Fryer on the side if you have more than one kitchen counter to use. You won't have to go through the trouble of finding cupboard space for it because you'll use it frequently enough to justify it.

The Ninja Foodi Dual Zone Air Fryer is a large but attractive appliance. Although it's a terrific appliance, my Ninja Foodi Max 9-in-1 Multi Cooker isn't as attractive. It has a polished and professional appearance that will go with just about any kitchen thanks to its matte finish and sleek handles, which match the machine's silver vent at the top. They are non-stick, so treat them like you would a typical non-stick frying pan, I should point you. Use silicone-tipped kitchen

tools to stir food or remove it from drawers.

You can configure the two drawers separately with various timings and temperatures using the Meal Sync setting, and the two drawers will cook side by side so they finish at the same time. The potatoes would start cooking earlier and the chicken would automatically begin cooking after 10 minutes if you were to cook potatoes for 30 minutes in one drawer and chicken for 20 minutes in the other.

You can specify the mode, timings, and temperature of one zone and match the other to it using the Match Zone feature. When I made cauliflower wings, I was able to evenly distribute the contents across both drawers, which worked nicely for me.

The outside of this machine is completely safe to touch without worrying that you'll burn yourself, and it won't heat up your kitchen. I wouldn't place this too close to a wall in order to give the machine room to control its temperature because the rear vent releases steam and cooking heat. Even though the drawers were undoubtedly hot to the touch, the drawer handles remained chilly. Before cleaning, allow the drawers to completely cool, just as you would a typical baking tray.

Each of the two crisper drawers included with the Ninja Foodi Dual Zone Air Fryer includes a non-stick crisper plate insert. By adding this, you may elevate the food you air fry, allowing air to move readily around it for a more crispy and fried-like outcome. The insert plates and the drawers may both be cleaned in the dishwasher, but they are also quite simple to wash by hand.

# Function buttons

Max crisp : Best for frozen items like French fries and chicken nuggets, MAX CRISP.

Air fry: Use the air fryer to add crunch and crisp to your meals while using little to no oil.

Roast: Use the appliance as an oven for tenderloins and other foods.

Reheat: Give leftovers a second life by softly reheating them, producing crunchy results. Dehydrate: Dehydrate fruits, vegetables, and meats for wholesome snacking.

Bake: Concoct opulent baked goods and deserts.

Activation buttons Control the drawer 1's output on the left (Zone 1). Control the drawer 2's output on the right (Zone 2).

Temp arrows: To change the cooking temperature before or while it is cooking, use the up and down arrows.

Time arrows: Before or during the cook cycle, use the up and down arrows to change the cook time in any function.

The sync button automatically synchronises the cook times so that both zones complete their tasks at the same time, even if their cook times differ.

The match button automatically adjusts zone 2 settings to zone 1 settings so that you can cook different dishes at the same function, temperature, and time while also cooking more of the same food.

Start/stop button: After deciding on the temperature and the cooking time, push the START/STOP button to begin cooking.

Power button: This button powers up the appliance, switches it off, and halts all cooking operations.

Standby mode: The device will go into standby mode after ten minutes without any interaction with the control panel. When in SYNC mode, the machine will

display

Hold mode: While the other zone waits for the times to synchronise, one zone will be cooking.

# Ahead of first use

1. Take off and throw away any tape, labels, or packing from the unit.
2. Take out all the accessories from the box and carefully study this handbook. Please pay close attention to all operational guidelines, precautions, and warnings to prevent accidents and damage to your property.
3. After washing the crisper plates and drawers in hot, soapy water, thoroughly rinse and dry them. Only the drawers and crisper plates can be put in the dishwasher. However, we advise hand-washing to increase the drawers' lifespan. NEVER clean the dishwasher's main unit.

# DualZone Technology

DualZone Technology uses two cooking zones to maximise variety when cooking. Regardless of the differing cook settings, the Syncfeature makes sure that both zones will be finished and ready to serve at the same time. See pages 9–12 for comprehensive instructions on how to use each function.

## Sync

When meals have varied cook times, temperatures, or even functions, to finish cooking at the same time:

1. Put ingredients in the drawers before inserting them into the unit.
2. Zone 1 will continue to be lit up. Choose your preferred cooking method. Set the temperature using the TEMP arrows, and the time with the TIME arrows.
3. 3 After choosing zone 2, choose the desired cooking function. Set the temperature using the TEMP arrows, and the time with the TIME arrows.
4. To start cooking in the zone with the longest cooking time, hit SYNC and then the START/STOP button. Hold will be shown on the otherzone. When both zones have the same amount of time left, the unit will beep and activate the second zone.

5. The appliance will beep when the cooking is finished, and "End" will appear on the display.
6. Remove the components by tipping them out or by using tongs or utensils with silicone tips. DON'T put a drawer on top of the appliance.

Match to prepare a larger quantity of the same food, or to prepare many foods at the same time, temperature, and function:

1. Put ingredients in the drawers before inserting them into the unit.
2. Zone 1 will continue to be lit up. Choose your preferred cooking method. Set the temperature using the TEMP arrows, and the time with the TIME arrows.
3. To transfer the settings from zone 1 to zone 2, press the MATCH button. then click start/stop to start the stove in both zones.
4. When cooking comes to an immediate stop, "End" will show up on both screens.
5. Remove ingredients by tipping them out or by using tongs or other objects with silicone tips.

## Beginning simultaneously in both zones but finishing at separate times:

1. After choosing zone 1, choose the desired function. To adjust the temperature, use the TEMP arrows.
2. To set the time, use the TIME arrows.
3. Repeat steps 1 and 2 for zone 2.
4. To start the cooking process in both zones, press the START/STOP button.

Ninja Foodi Dual Zone Air Fryer Cookbook | 11

NOTE: You can STOP A ZONE if you decide the food in one of the zones is finished cooking before the allotted cook time has passed.

After choosing that zone, press START/STOP.

5. The device will beep and the word "End" will appear on the display when cooking is finished in each zone.

6. Remove ingredients by tipping them out or by using tongs or other objects with silicone tips.

## Max Crisp

1. Before inserting the drawer into the unit, install the crisper plate, then add the ingredients.

2. By default, the device will be in zone 1. (to usezone 2 instead, select zone 2). ChooseMAX CRISP.

3. To set the time in 1-minute increments up to 30 minutes, use the TIME arrows. To start cooking, press the START/STOP button.

4. The appliance will beep and the word "End" will show on the display when cooking is finished.

5. Remove ingredients by tipping them out or by using tongs or utensils with silicone tips.

## Air fryer

1. Install the crisper plate in the drawer, add the contents, and then put the drawer into the unit.

2. By default, the device will be in zone 1. . Choose AIR FRY.

3. To set the desired temperature, use the TEMP arrows.

4. To specify the time in 1-minute intervals up to an hour, use the TIME arrows. Simply push the START/STOP button to begin cooking. NOTE: You can remove the drawer during cooking and shake or toss the ingredients for evening crisping.

5. The appliance will beep and "End" will show up on the display when cooking is finished.

6. Remove ingredients by tipping them out or by using tongs or other objects with silicone tips.

### Roast

1. After placing the ingredients in the drawer and inserting it into the unit, install the crisper plate in the drawer (optional).
2. The device will automatically enter zone 1 Choose ROAST.
3. To set the required temperature, use the TEMP arrows.
4. To set the time in 1-minute increments up to 1 hour and in 5-minute increments from 1 to 4 hours, use the TIME arrows. Simply push the START/STOP button to begin cooking..
5. The appliance will beep and "End" will show up on the display when cooking is finished.
6. Remove ingredients by using silicone-tipped tools or by tipping them out.

## Reheat

1. Before placing the ingredients in the drawer and inserting it into the unit, install the crisper plate in the drawer (optional).
2. The device will automatically enter zone 1 (to use zone 2 instead, select zone 2). Select REHEAT.
3. To set the required temperature, use the TEMP arrows.
4. To specify the time in 1-minute intervals up to an hour, use the TIME arrows. In order to start warming, press the START/STOP button.
5. The machine will beep and "End" will show up on the display after warming is finished.
6. Remove ingredients by using silicone-tipped tools or by tipping them out.

## Dehydrate

1. Put the ingredients in the drawer in a single layer Install the crisper plate in the drawer over the contents, and then arrange more items on top of that.
2. By default, the device will be in zone 1. Select DEHYDRATE. The display will show the current temperature by default. To set the preferred temperature, use the TEMP

arrows.

3. To set the time in 15-minute increments between 1 and 12 hours, use the TIME arrows. To start dehydrating, Simply push the START/STOP button to begin cooking..

4. The appliance will beep and the word "End" will show on the display when cooking is finished.

5. Remove ingredients by tipping them out or by using tongs or other objects with silicone tips.

### Bake

1. After placing the ingredients in the drawer and inserting it into the unit, install the crisper plate in the drawer (optional).

2. The device will automatically enter zone 1. Choose BAKE. NOTE: Decrease the temperature by 10°C when converting recipes for traditional ovens.

3. To set the required temperature, use the TEMP arrows.

4. To set the time in 1-minute increments up to 1 hour and in 5-minute increments from 1 to 4 hours, use the TIME arrows. To start cooking, Simply push the START/STOP button to begin cooking..

5. The appliance will beep and "End" will show up on the display when cooking is finished.

6. Remove ingredients by tipping them out or by using tongs or utensils with silicone tips.

## Cleaning & maintenance

Cleaning and upkeep After each usage, the appliance needs to be completely cleaned. Remove the plug from the device and let it cool completely before cleaning. Method for Cleaning a Part or Accessory Wipe the main unit and the control panel with a moist cloth to clean them. Primary Unit NOTE: The main unit MUST NEVER be submerged in water or any other liquid. NEVER clean a dishwasher's main unit or drawer. These can be hand-washed or put in the dishwasher. After using, air-dry or dry all pieces with a towel if they were hand-washed. We advise hand-washing the drawers to increase their lifespan. Place the crisper plates or drawers in a sink full of warm, soapy water and let them

soak if food residue has trapped on them.

## Helpful tips

1. For consistent browning, make sure that the ingredients are put on the bottom of the drawer in an even layer without touching one another. Make careful to shake the ingredients halfway through the designated cooking time if they are overlapping.
2. You can alter the cooking temperature and duration at any moment. Simply choose the zone you want to change, then use the TEMP or TIME arrows to change the temperature or time.
3. Decrease the temperature by 10°C in order to adapt recipes from your regular oven. To prevent overcooking, periodically check your food.
4. Sometimes, the air fryer's fan will fling light meals everywhere. Secure things using cocktail sticks to prevent this, such as the top slice of bread on a sandwich.
5. For consistent, crisp results, the crisper plates elevate the ingredients in the drawers so that air can circulate under and around them.
6. To start cooking right away after choosing a cooking option, push the START/STOP button. The device will operate at its standard temperature and time.
7. Use at least 1 tablespoon of oil when cooking fresh veggies and potatoes for the best results. To obtain the required level of crispiness, add additional oil as needed.
8. For best results, monitor the cooking process frequently and remove the item after the required level of brownness has been reached. We advise checking the internal temperature of meat and fish with an instant-read thermometer. To prevent overcooking, remove food from the heat as soon as the cook time is up.
9. To achieve the best results and prevent overcooking, remove food as soon as the cook time is up.

# Frequently Asked Questions

How can I change the time or the temperature in a specific zone?

Use the TEMP arrows to change the temperature or the TIME arrows to change the time after choosing the active zone.

How can I change the time or the temperature when using dual zones?

Use the TEMP arrows to change the temperature or the TIME arrows to change the time after choosing the desired zone.

Does the device require pre-heating?

It is not necessary to pre-heat the device.

Can I prepare different dishes without worrying about cross-contamination in each zone?

Yes, each zones have independent heating elements and fans and are self-contained.

How can the countdown be paused?

When you take the drawers out of the unit, the countdown timer will automatically pause. If the drawer is not reinserted in the next two minutes, the machine will shut off on its own.

When using both zones, how can I stop one zone?

Press the zone button first, then START/STOP to stop one zone. Simply push the START/Halt button to stop both zones.

Is it okay to place the drawer on my worktop?

The drawer will warm up while you're cooking. Handle with care and only place on surfaces resistant to heat.

In a Ninja Foodi dual zone Air fryer AF300UK, what can you cook?

From mouthwatering fishcakes, burgers, and sausages to thick-cut fries. Through the even circulation of extremely hot air, air frying removes excess moisture from food and imparts a wonderful golden finish. Max Crisp: cook in minutes from frozen to crispy.

What caused the screen to go black?

The device is set to standby. Activate the power button.

# Chapter 1: Breakfast

## Air Fryer Toasted Bagels

Prep Time: 1 Min
Cook Time: 15 Mins   Serves: 2

### Ingredients:

- 2 Frozen Bagels
- 2 Tbsp Soft Cheese
- 1 Tsp Butter

### Directions:

1. Using a vegetable knife, slice your frozen bagels in half.
2. Add your frozen bagels into the air fryer and cook for 5 minutes at 180°C.
3. When the air fryer beeps, remove the toasted bagels, and load them up with your favourite toppings. Load onto a plate and enjoy!

### Nutritional Value (Amount per Serving):

Calories: 301; Fat: 6.03; Carb: 49.24; Protein: 12.58

## Air Fryer Quesadilla

Prep Time: 4 Mins
Cook Time: 6 Mins   Serves: 4

### Ingredients:

- 8 Tortilla Wraps
- Egg Wash
- 3 Tbsp Salsa
- 100 g Grated Mexican Cheese
- heese Quesadilla Filling:
- 1 Can Black Beans
- 150g Frozen Sweetcorn
- 250 g Grated Frozen Cheddar Cheese
- 2 Tbsp Sour Cream
- 2 Tsp Garlic Powder
- 1 Tbsp Mexican Seasoning

### Directions:

1. Load filling ingredients into a mixing bowl and mix well with a fork.
2. Load the filling over one of your tortilla wraps.
3. Add grated cheese over.

4. Spread salsa over another wrap with a knife and then press the salsa down over the grated cheese so that you have a sandwich.
5. Cover the top with egg wash and then load it up with cocktail sticks so that it can't move.
6. Load into the air fryer and cook for 4 minutes at 180°C.
7. When it beeps, remove cocktail sticks, flip and add extra egg wash. Cook for a further 2 minutes at 200°C.
8. Slice and serve with extra salsa.
9. Rinse and repeat until you have used all your tortilla wraps and are out of filling.

**Nutritional Value (Amount per Serving):**

Calories: 700; Fat: 29.03; Carb: 78.11; Protein: 30.78

## My Crisp Bacon Cheese Wrapped Breast With Asparagus

Prep Time: 10 Mins
Cook Time: 30 Mins        Serves: 2

### Ingredients:

- 2 Chicken breasts
- 2 Slices Smoked Cheese
- 4 Slices Streaky Bacon
- 2 tbls Grated Chedder Cheese1 Red Sweet Bell Pepper sliced
- 2 tbls Grated Chedder Cheese

### Directions:

1. Steam both chickens first for about 20 minutes
2. Next add the two chicken breasts on grease proof paper. Wrap the smoked Cheese slice around the chicken, then wrap the 2 slices Streaky Bacon around each chicken
3. Make a fold in between both breasts so separate. Then carefully add to the Air fryer for 10 minutes on 175°C.
4. Arrange the Asparagus on grease proof paper and then add the sliced red pepper
5. Next add the Grated Cheese on top with a little spray of oil. Add on the paper to the air fryer for 10 minutes on 190°C.
6. Take out the chicken when done and add to both serving dish or plates also the Asparagus add to plates

7. Have these with Salad, Homemade Chips or crisp roast potatoes.

**Nutritional Value (Amount per Serving):**

Calories: 820; Fat: 54.45; Carb: 5.98; Protein: 72.89

## Air Fryer Soft Boiled Eggs

Prep Time: 1 Min
Cook Time: 10 Mins      Serves: 3

### Ingredients:

- 6 Eggs
- Sea Salt

### Directions:

1. Load eggs into the air fryer basket, making sure none of them are cracked.
2. Set the temperature to 120°C and cook for 10 minutes.
3. When the air fryer beeps quickly load into egg cups and slice the tops off. Serve with toast or cucumber/carrot sticks.

**Nutritional Value (Amount per Serving):**

Calories: 259; Fat: 19.28; Carb: 2.03; Protein: 17.93

## Air Fryer Crumpets

Prep Time: 1 Min
Cook Time: 3 Mins      Serves: 2

### Ingredients:

- 4 Warburton Crumpets
- 2 Tsp Butter
- 2 Tsp Strawberry Jam optional
- 2 Tsp Soft Cheese optional
- 2 Tsp Chicken Liver Pate optional

### Directions:

1. Place up to four crumpets into the air fryer basket and make sure they are not on top of one another. Set the air fryer cook time to 2 minutes and the temperature to 180°C.
2. When the air fryer beeps add butter on top and cook for a further 1 minute at 200°C.

3. Serve as the butter drips down into the crumpet holes.

**Nutritional Value (Amount per Serving):**

Calories: 237; Fat: 10.56; Carb: 27.47; Protein: 8

## Air Fried Beef Sausage Rolls

Prep Time: 5 Mins
Cook Time: 10 Mins    Serves: 2

**Ingredients:**

- 1 packet frozen puff pastry
- 8 Beef sausage I used

**Directions:**

1. I rolled out the packet (kilo)
2. Took the skins of a packet of 8 beef sausages
3. Roll the sausage meat in some flour. put the onto the pastry and rolled pastry over the sausage and cut along the edge. I did this until I'd used all the pastry and sausages. I sprayed the crisping plate on my ninja and put sausage rolls all over. Brushed them with milk and cooked on air-fry 190°C for 5 mins. Then checked they were not burnt and put them on for another 5 mins.

**Nutritional Value (Amount per Serving):**

Calories: 277; Fat: 21.37; Carb: 12.26; Protein: 8.44

## Air-Fried Eggs

Prep Time: 2 Mins
Cook Time: 8 Mins    Serves: 2

**Ingredients:**

- 2 eggs
- Bowl cold water

**Directions:**

1. Air-fry your eggs for 8min at 150°C for soft yolks
2. Cold water bath them when they come out to stop the cooking process. Enjoy !

**Nutritional Value (Amount per Serving):**

Calories: 130; Fat: 9.64; Carb: 1.02; Protein: 8.97

## Air Fried Bacon And Poached Eggs

Prep Time: 10 Mins
Cook Time: 14 Mins      Serves: 2

**Ingredients:**

- 12 rashers bacon
- 4 hen eggs
- 1 piece buttered toast (optional)
- Vinegar

**Directions:**

1. Boil cold water in a medium sized saucepan, once boiling - put on a simmer and add lots of Vinegar, I used Malt Vinegar.
2. Put Air Fryer on to - a temperature of 200°C and place bacon rashers in 2 stuck together and air fry on the One sides for 7 minutes and then turn the bacon rashers over and air fry for a further 7 minutes.
3. When the Air Fryer is down to the last 4 minutes of its final cooking time - then crack 2 eggs into a small Dessert Bowl and then place in the non boiling hot water with Vinegar in - and then do the same with the final 2 eggs - keep the hob still on a simmer and the eggs will only need 2 or 3 minutes.
4. Use a slotted spoon too drain Vinegar and water off of the poached eggs and let dry on Kitchen Roll and then add too serving plate and then add the cooked bacon too the plate. Done.

**Nutritional Value (Amount per Serving):**

Calories: 416; Fat: 29.93; Carb: 13.46; Protein: 23.32

# Air Fryer Baked Smores

Prep Time: 5 Mins
Cook Time: 13 Mins     Serves: 4

## Ingredients:

- 8 Tbsp Mini Marshmallows
- 200 g Squares Galaxy Chocolate
- 8 Extra Graham Crackers for serving
- Graham Cracker Cookie Dough
- 130 g Self Raising Flour
- 8 Graham Crackers
- 4 Tbsp Butter
- 4 Tbsp Caster Sugar
- 1 Medium Egg
- 1 Tsp Vanilla Essence

## Directions:

1. Place 1tbp of butter into each of the ramekins and air fry for 3 minutes at 180°C.
2. Whilst the butter is in the air fryer, add all other cookie dough ingredients into a bowl, breaking up the Graham Crackers with your hands as you do it.
3. When butter has melted stir it into the dough and then divide equally between the four ramekins.
4. Optional – air fry for 5 minutes at 180°C to turn the dough into a baked cookie. Or if you like sticky dough then jump ahead to adding in the chocolate squares.
5. Place as many mini marshmallows on top of each ramekin that will fit and then air fry for 5 minutes at 180°C or until the marshmallows are golden.
6. Then serve with extra Graham Crackers.

## Nutritional Value (Amount per Serving):

Calories: 859; Fat: 43.41; Carb: 102.29; Protein: 15.58

# Chapter 2: Vegetables

## Air Fryer Frozen Breaded Mushrooms

Prep Time: 1 Min
Cook Time: 10 Mins            Serves: 4

### Ingredients:

- 500 g Frozen Breaded Mushrooms

### Directions:

1. Open the breaded mushrooms bag into a mixing bowl or any large bowl.
2. Grab the breaded mushrooms one by one making sure the excess breadcrumbs stay in the bowl and place them into the air fryer. Cook the breaded mushrooms in the air fryer, for 10 minutes at 180°C.

### Nutritional Value (Amount per Serving):

Calories: 296; Fat: 0.99; Carb: 75.37; Protein: 9.58

## Padron Peppers

Prep Time: 2 Mins
Cook Time: 8 Mins            Serves: 2

### Ingredients:

- 200 gr pardon peppers
- 1 tbsp olive oil
- Salt to test

### Directions:

1. Wash the peppers in a bowl and drain them.
2. I used an Air Frier to fried them. Set the air frier at 200°C for 8 minutes. Shake the basket half way.
3. Add salt and ready to serve.

### Nutritional Value (Amount per Serving):

Calories: 100; Fat: 6.95; Carb: 9.46; Protein: 2

# Air Fryer Kohlrabi Fries

Prep Time: 3 Mins  
Cook Time: 10 Mins     Serves: 2

### Ingredients:

- 1 large kohlrabi
- Olive oil
- Paprika
- Salt

### Directions:

1. Peel and cut your kohlrabi into chips. Wash and drain.
2. Season well with salt and paprika. Give a good drizzle of olive oil and toss to cover. Cook in the air fryer at 200°C for 10 minutes until crisp. Enjoy

### Nutritional Value (Amount per Serving):

Calories: 71; Fat: 7.2; Carb: 2.33; Protein: 0.62

# Air Fryer Corn On The Cob

Prep Time: 2 Mins  
Cook Time: 10 Mins     Serves: 3

### Ingredients:

- 3 ears sweet corn
- Butter

### Directions:

1. Prepare the corn by removing the husks and dividing each ear into thirds.
2. Rub each section with butter and place in air fryer basket. Set to air-fry at 200°C for 10 minutes
3. After 10 minutes it's ready! Super easy and tasty. Enjoy!

### Nutritional Value (Amount per Serving):

Calories: 147; Fat: 4.26; Carb: 27.2; Protein: 4.76

## Air Fryer Radishes

Prep Time: 2 Mins
Cook Time: 15 Mins         Serves: 1

### Ingredients:

- Small Radishes
- Dried oregano
- To taste Salt
- To taste Ground black pepper
- Drizzle olive oil

### Directions:

1. Preheat air fryer to 200°C.
2. Mix the Radishes well with all the ingredients.
3. Air-fry for 15 minutes, shaking basket occasionally.
4. Serve immediately. Sprinkle with more salt if needed.

### Nutritional Value (Amount per Serving):

Calories: 142; Fat: 13.67; Carb: 5.57; Protein: 1.08

## Air Fryer Cabbage

Prep Time: 5 Mins
Cook Time: 12 Mins         Serves: 4

### Ingredients:

- 1 head green cabbage cored and sliced
- 1 tablespoon olive oil
- ¾ teaspoon ground ginger
- salt and pepper to taste

### Directions:

1. Preheat air fryer to 190°C.
2. In a bowl, combine cabbage, olive oil, ground ginger, salt and pepper.
3. Add the cabbage to the air fryer basket and air fry for 8-12 minutes, turning a couple of times during cooking.

### Nutritional Value (Amount per Serving):

Calories: 79; Fat: 3.64; Carb: 11.76; Protein: 2.28

## Air Fryer Asparagus

Prep Time: 5 Mins
Cook Time: 8 Mins    Serves: 4

### Ingredients:

- 1 Bunch of asparagus
- Cooking spray
- Salt

### Directions:

1. Preheat the air fryer to 200°C.
2. Trim, rinse and dry asparagus spears.
3. Lightly spray with cooking spray and sprinkle with salt.
4. Place the asparagus spears in single layer inside the air fryer basket
5. Cook for 5-8 mins (5 mins for thinner stems and 8 for thicker stems).
6. Remove from air fryer and serve.

### Nutritional Value (Amount per Serving):

Calories: 54; Fat: 0.33; Carb: 10.48; Protein: 5.65

## Cajun Air-Fried Potatoes

Prep Time: 3 Mins
Cook Time: 14 Mins    Serves: 2

### Ingredients:

- as needed Potatoes, cut into bite size cubes,
- Salt to taste
- Cracked black pepper to taste
- Cajun spice to taste
- 1 small drizzle of olive oil

### Directions:

1. Mix all the ingredients together in a bowl. Let it sit in the marinade for 30 minutes.
2. Preheat air fryer to 200°C.
3. Toss the potatoes in and air-fry for 11-14 minutes or until cooked through and crispy.

### Nutritional Value (Amount per Serving):

Calories: 220; Fat: 7.31; Carb: 36.3; Protein: 4.34

# Rosemary Roast Potatoes Air Fryer Style

Prep Time: 2 Mins
Cook Time: 10 Mins    Serves: 4

### Ingredients:

- 2 Large Potatoes
- 1Tsp Rosemary
- 1Tbsp Olive Oil
- Salt & Pepper

### Directions:

1. Peel your potatoes and cut them into roast potato shapes.
2. Place them in your Air Fryer for 10 minutes on a 180°C temperature with a tablespoon of olive oil.
3. Once cooked place them in a mixing bowl and sprinkle with the rosemary and the salt and pepper.
4. Mix well and then serve.

### Nutritional Value (Amount per Serving):

Calories: 177; Fat: 3.59; Carb: 33.38; Protein: 3.9

# My Salt Rainbow Peppered Buttered Asparagus

Prep Time: 2 Mins
Cook Time: 11 Mins    Serves: 2

### Ingredients:

- 1 Bunch Asparagus trim off the end bits
- Pieces Butter
- Salt
- Cracked Rainbow Pepper

### Directions:

1. Trim off the end bits and add par heat paper to the Airfry basket.
2. Add the dots of Butter all over the Asparagus
3. Next add the salt all over and the cracked Rainbow peppercorns
4. Airfry on 200°C for 9 minutes turn them over and add back for a further 2 minutes. Take out and add to a serving dish. And serve

**Nutritional Value (Amount per Serving):**

Calories: 45; Fat: 3.9; Carb: 2.2; Protein: 0.72

## Air-Fried Onion With Balsamic Vinegar

Prep Time: 2 Mins
Cook Time: 15 Mins     Serves: 1

**Ingredients:**

- 1 big onion
- 1 tablespoon balsamic vinegar
- 1 tablespoon oil (olive oil or vegetable oil)

**Directions:**

1. Turn the air fryer on while you prepare the onions.
2. Remove the skin and slice the onion into evenly thick slices.
3. Place them in the air-fryer.
4. Mix the vinegar and oil in a small bowl and brush the onion slices with the mixture. Cook for 10-15 minutes on 180°C.
5. Sprinkle salt and enjoy!

**Nutritional Value (Amount per Serving):**

Calories: 178; Fat: 13.71; Carb: 13; Protein: 1.29

# Chapter 3: Meats

# Air Fryer Pork Loin

Prep Time: 3 Mins
Cook Time: 1 Hr 5 Mins    Serves: 4

### Ingredients:

- 1.5 kg Pork Loin
- 1 Tbsp Pork Seasoning
- 1 Tbsp Bouquet Garni
- Salt & Pepper

### Directions:

1. Place your pork loin over your air fryer and check to see if it will fit. If it doesn't trim a little off and put the leftovers aside for later for some air fryer pork loin chops.
2. Load seasonings into a small bowl and mix.
3. Add your seasonings around the top and sides of the pork loin. Reserving a little for the bottom later.
4. Place your pork loin in the air fryer and cook for 35 minutes at 180°C. Turn and sprinkle the rest of the seasoning. Cook for a further 30 minutes at the same time and temp.
5. Slice your air fryer pork loin and enjoy!

### Nutritional Value (Amount per Serving):

Calories: 792; Fat: 41.63; Carb: 1.12; Protein: 96.74

# Spanish Seasoned Pork Loin Steaks

Prep Time: 5 Mins
Cook Time: 25 Mins    Serves: 4

### Ingredients:

- 4 pork loins
- 12 tbls Spanish mixed seasoning
- 1 Garlic clove crushed
- 2 tbls Bread crumbs
- Spray oil

### Directions:

1. Mix the breadcrumbs and seasoning together and the crushed Garlic clove. Mix then add to the pork loins and marinate for 2 hours

2. Spray with spray oil and add a piece of parchment paper to the bottom of the airfry basket then add the loin to Air fry for 15 minutes turning over and spray again for 10 minutes 175°C.
3. Take out and Serve with whatever you want. Enjoy

**Nutritional Value (Amount per Serving):**

Calories: 502; Fat: 21.52; Carb: 26.24; Protein: 43.4

## Air Fried Fish With Sweet Chilli Leafs

Prep Time: 1 Min
Cook Time: 15 Mins          Serves: 1

**Ingredients:**

- Half pack mixed leafs
- 4 battered fish strips
- Sweet chilli sauce

**Directions:**

1. Put fish in air fryer for 15mins at 180°C and tear half bag of mixed leafs in a bowl
2. Once fish is cook add sauce to bowl and mix well I have 2 to 3 squeezes of sauce then put fish on top so they stay crispy enjoy

**Nutritional Value (Amount per Serving):**

Calories: 908; Fat: 57.75; Carb: 6.15; Protein: 88.5

## My Air fryer Crispy Ham And Cheese Rolls

Prep Time: 3 Mins
Cook Time: 12 Mins          Serves: 2

**Ingredients:**

- 2 rolls
- 4 slices ham
- 4 slices favourite cheese
- 1 tomato sliced
- Melted butter to brush rolls

**Directions:**

1. Cut rolls in half butter lightly
2. Add ham tomato and cheese, lightly coat with more butter on the outside

3. Place in air fryer at 200°C for 12-15 mins checking after 20 minutes, cook until its crispy enough for our own taste....and enjoy

**Nutritional Value (Amount per Serving):**

Calories: 446; Fat: 27.86; Carb: 23; Protein: 25.63

## Air Fryer Sausages

Prep Time: 3 Mins
Cook Time: 10 Mins          Serves: 8

**Ingredients:**

- 8 sausages

**Directions:**

1. Preheat the air fryer to 180°C.
2. Pierce each sausage with a knife or fork.
3. Lay sausages in the air fryer basket.
4. Cook for 10 minutes, checking on them and turning them over after 5 minutes.

**Nutritional Value (Amount per Serving):**

Calories: 73; Fat: 5.15; Carb: 2.79; Protein: 5.25

## Air Fryer Meatballs

Prep Time: 10 Mins
Cook Time: 7 Mins           Serves:

**Ingredients:**

- 500g lean beef mince, (1 pound)
- 1 clove garlic, crushed
- 1 tsp dried mixed herbs
- 1 egg
- 1tbsp breadcrumbs, (optional)

**Directions:**

1. Mix all ingredients together until well combined.
2. Using your hands, form small round balls (this recipe makes about 16, depending on size of meatballs)
3. Place meatballs in air fryer and cook at 180°C for 7 minutes. Check half way through and turn over if necessary.
4. If you want to add a sauce, once the meatballs are cooked transfer them

to an ovenproof dish/pan that will fit in the Air fryer. Pour your choice of tomato sauce on top and place container in Air fryer tray. Cook at 180°C for about 6-8 minutes, or until the sauce is warmed through.
5. Serve with spaghetti and melted cheese.

### Nutritional Value (Amount per Serving):

Calories: 799; Fat: 38.2; Carb: 2.02; Protein: 111.76

## Air Fryer Pork Chops

Prep Time: 5 Mins
Cook Time: 12 Mins     Serves: 1

### Ingredients:

- 1 pork chop
- 1/2 tbsp olive oil
- 1/2 tbsp seasoning

### Directions:

1. Preheat the air fryer to 200°C.
2. Brush oil on each side of the pork chop.
3. Add seasoning and rub it in evenly all over.
4. Place pork chop in the preheated air fryer and set the timer for 12 minutes. Turn the pork chop over at around the 6 minute mark.
5. Check the pork chop is cooked all the way through - it should be golden brown on the outside and juices should run clear.

### Nutritional Value (Amount per Serving):

Calories: 402; Fat: 24.16; Carb: 2.49; Protein: 40.4

## Air Fryer Bacon

Prep Time: 2 Mins
Cook Time: 10 Mins     Serves: 2

### Ingredients:

- 2 rashers smoked bacon
- Alternatively
- 2 rashers streaky bacon

### Directions:

1. Preheat your air fryer to 200°C for a couple of minutes.

Ninja Foodi Dual Zone Air Fryer Cookbook | 35

2. Place your bacon of choice in a single layer in your air fryer basket. It is ok if it overlaps slightly, or the edges fold over slightly.
3. You may need to repeat the cooking a couple of times if you have a lot of bacon, or a smaller air fryer basket (like I currently do!).
4. Cooking times are as follows:
Smoked streaky bacon rashers – 200°C – 11 minutes.
Smoked bacon rashers – 200°C – 10 minutes.
Smoked bacon medallions – 200°C – 8 minutes.

### Nutritional Value (Amount per Serving):

Calories: 1456; Fat: 138.63; Carb: 29.68; Protein: 50.15

## Crispy Air Fryer Bacon

Prep Time: 5 Mins
Cook Time: 10 Mins    Serves: 8

### Ingredients:

- 340 g thick-cut bacon

### Directions:

1. Lay bacon inside air fryer basket in a single layer.
2. Set air fryer to 200°C and cook until crispy, about 10 minutes. (You can check halfway through and rearrange slices with tongs.)

### Nutritional Value (Amount per Serving):

Calories: 132; Fat: 12.55; Carb: 2.69; Protein: 4.54

## Air Fryer Steak Bites

Prep Time: 5 Mins
Cook Time: 10 Mins    Serves: 4

### Ingredients:

- 500 g Steak Rib eye, Sirloin, or any good cut.
- 1 teaspoon Garlic Powder
- ½ teaspoon Ginger powder
- ½ teaspoon Dried Parsley
- ½ teaspoon Black pepper or to taste

- Salt to taste
- 1 tablespoon Olive oil or Garlic Butter
- 1 tablespoon Fresh Parsley finely chopped
- 2 tablespoons Butter
- 1 teaspoon Garlic minced

### Directions:

1. First, make the garlic herb butter by mixing the butter, garlic, and parsley together. Wrap in baking paper, or clingfilm, and put it in the fridge to chill.
2. Next, cut the steak into cube bite size.
3. Add the garlic powder, black pepper, ginger, salt, parsley, and oil to the steak cuts and mix till well combined.
4. Arrange the steak bites in the air fryer basket in a single layer without overlapping.
5. Air fry at 190°C for 4-5 minutes. Flip the steak bites using a tong (or shake) then continue to air fry it for another 4-5 minutes.
6. Take the steak bites out of the air fryer and immediately add the garlic butter to it.
7. Serve and enjoy as a snack or with any side of choice for a complete meal.

### Nutritional Value (Amount per Serving):

Calories: 293; Fat: 21; Carb: 1; Protein: 25

## Air Fryer Frozen Sausages

Prep Time: 5 Mins
Cook Time: 12 Mins      Serves: 4

### Ingredients:

- 4 Sausages chicken, beef, Pork

### Directions:

1. Put the frozen sausages in the air fryer basket.
2. Air fry at a temperature of 160°C for 4 minutes.
3. Bring air fryer basket out and use a spatula to separate the sausages into individual pieces.
4. Put the basket back in the air fryer and cook sausages at 160°C for 15- 20 minutes (flipping them with a tong halfway into cooking) or until cooked.
5. Bring out the sausages and serve.

### Nutritional Value (Amount per Serving):

Calories: 1166; Fat: 82.37; Carb: 44.63; Protein: 84.05

# Chapter 4: Poultry

## Air-Fried Chicken

Prep Time: 2 Mins
Cook Time: 45 Mins   Serves: 4

### Ingredients:

- 1 whole Chicken, chopped
- 1 T Fish sauce

### Directions:

1. Pour fish sauce to the chicken.
2. Put to air-fryer for 45 minutes at 180°C.
3. Flip the chicken until all the sides are golden brown.

### Nutritional Value (Amount per Serving):

Calories: 266; Fat: 6.44; Carb: 0.16; Protein: 48.71

## 10-Minute Chicken Pizza

Prep Time: 2 Mins
Cook Time: 10 Mins   Serves: 1

### Ingredients:

- 2 fillets chicken
- 2 tsp tomato passata
- 1 pinch oregano
- 1 small onion
- 1 couple of slices of ham
- 2 small slabs of gorgonzola cheese
- Black pepper

### Directions:

1. Place all of them in the air fryer at 200°C for 10 minutes. Enjoy!!

### Nutritional Value (Amount per Serving):

Calories: 661; Fat: 22.25; Carb: 13.94; Protein: 98.04

## Chicken Wings, Drumsticks And Thighs In Air Fryer

Prep Time: 5 Mins
Cook Time: 28 Mins       Serves: 4

### Ingredients:

- 1 kg chicken parts (wings - wingette and drumette, thighs, drumstick)
- Pinch salt
- Pinch black pepper

### Directions:

1. Season the chicken part with salt and pepper. No need to add oil!
2. Place in the air fryer
3. Select the option air fry, on 200°C and cook for 25-28 minutes!

### Nutritional Value (Amount per Serving):

Calories: 294; Fat: 9.33; Carb: 1.1; Protein: 48.7

## Reheat Fried Chicken In Air Fryer

Prep Time: 1 Min
Cook Time: 16 Mins       Serves: 4

### Ingredients:

- Leftover Fried Chicken
- Extra Virgin Olive Oil Spray optional

### Directions:

1. Place the frozen pieces of KFC Chicken into the air fryer basket and reheat for 16 minutes at 160°C.
2. When it beeps following my notes below, check to see if the chicken is fully reheated.
3. Serve with your favourite sides.

### Nutritional Value (Amount per Serving):

Calories: 157; Fat: 14.79; Carb: 0; Protein: 5.7

## Tyson Chicken Wings In Air Fryer

Prep Time: 1 Min
Cook Time: 10 Mins    Serves: 2

### Ingredients:

- 1 Pack Frozen Tyson Chicken Wings

### Directions:

1. Remove frozen chicken wings from the packaging.
2. Place into your air fryer basket making sure that the chicken wings are not overcrowded.
3. Cook for 10 minutes at 180°C. Turning halfway through so that you get an even cook on your chicken wings.
4. Serve with your favourite wing dipping sauce.

### Nutritional Value (Amount per Serving):

Calories: 31; Fat: 1.84; Carb: 0.48; Protein: 2.85

## Air Fryer Tgi Friday Boneless Chicken Wings

Prep Time: 1 Min
Cook Time: 17 Mins    Serves: 4

### Ingredients:

- 1 Box TGI Friday Boneless Chicken Wings

### Directions:

1. Load into the air fryer basket your frozen boneless wings. Set the temperature to 180c and the cook time to 12 minutes.
2. When it beeps add your buffalo sauce frozen sachets and air fry for a further 5 minutes at 200°C.
3. When the air fryer beeps, toss the boneless chicken wings in the buffalo sauce, and serve.

### Nutritional Value (Amount per Serving):

Calories: 239; Fat: 14.37; Carb: 3.79; Protein: 22.31

## Air Fryer Chicken Wrapped In Bacon

Prep Time: 3 Mins
Cook Time: 15 Mins    Serves: 6

### Ingredients:

- 6 Rashers Unsmoked Back Bacon
- 1 Small Chicken Breast
- 1Tbsp Garlic Soft Cheese

### Directions:

1. Chop up your chicken breast into six bite sized pieces.
2. Lay out your bacon rashers and spread them with a small layer of soft cheese.
3. Place your chicken on top of the cheese and roll them up. Secure them with a cocktail stick.
4. Place them in the Air Fryer for 15 minutes on a 180°C heat.

### Nutritional Value (Amount per Serving):

Calories: 99; Fat: 5.98; Carb: 0.32; Protein: 10.64

## Air Fryer Piri Piri Chicken Legs

Prep Time: 5 Mins
Cook Time: 22 Mins    Serves: 4

### Ingredients:

- 4 chicken legs
- 2 tsp Piri Piri spice mix
- 120g Piri Piri marinade sauce (approx)

### Directions:

1. Add the spice mix and sauce to the raw chicken legs. Leave them to marinate for around 30 minutes.
2. Transfer to the air fryer basket and cook at 190°C for 22 minutes.
3. Turn the chicken legs at the halfway mark.
4. The chicken legs are ready when the juices run clear and the internal temperature is 75°C–use a meat thermometer if necessary.

### Nutritional Value (Amount per Serving):

Calories: 345; Fat: 11.19; Carb: 4.87; Protein: 52.55

# Hot Juicy Air Fried Chicken Wings

Prep Time: 10 Mins
Cook Time: 35 Mins     Serves: 6

## Ingredients:

- 2 kg Chicken Wings
- 1 Tsp Chiltepin Chilli Powder
- 1 Tsp Rock Salt
- 1 Tsp Onion Powder
- 1 Tsp Garlic Powder
- 1 Tsp Coriander Powder
- 1 Tsp Lemon Grass Powder
- 1 Tsp White Pepper
- 1 Tsp Turmeric

## Directions:

1. Cut apart the three sections of the chicken wings & discard the tips.
2. Combine all spices in spice grinder.
3. Cover wings with spices and mix well.
4. Cook in air fryer at 200°C for 35 minutes, tossing every 5 minutes.

## Nutritional Value (Amount per Serving):

Calories: 426; Fat: 11.83; Carb: 1.36; Protein: 73.46

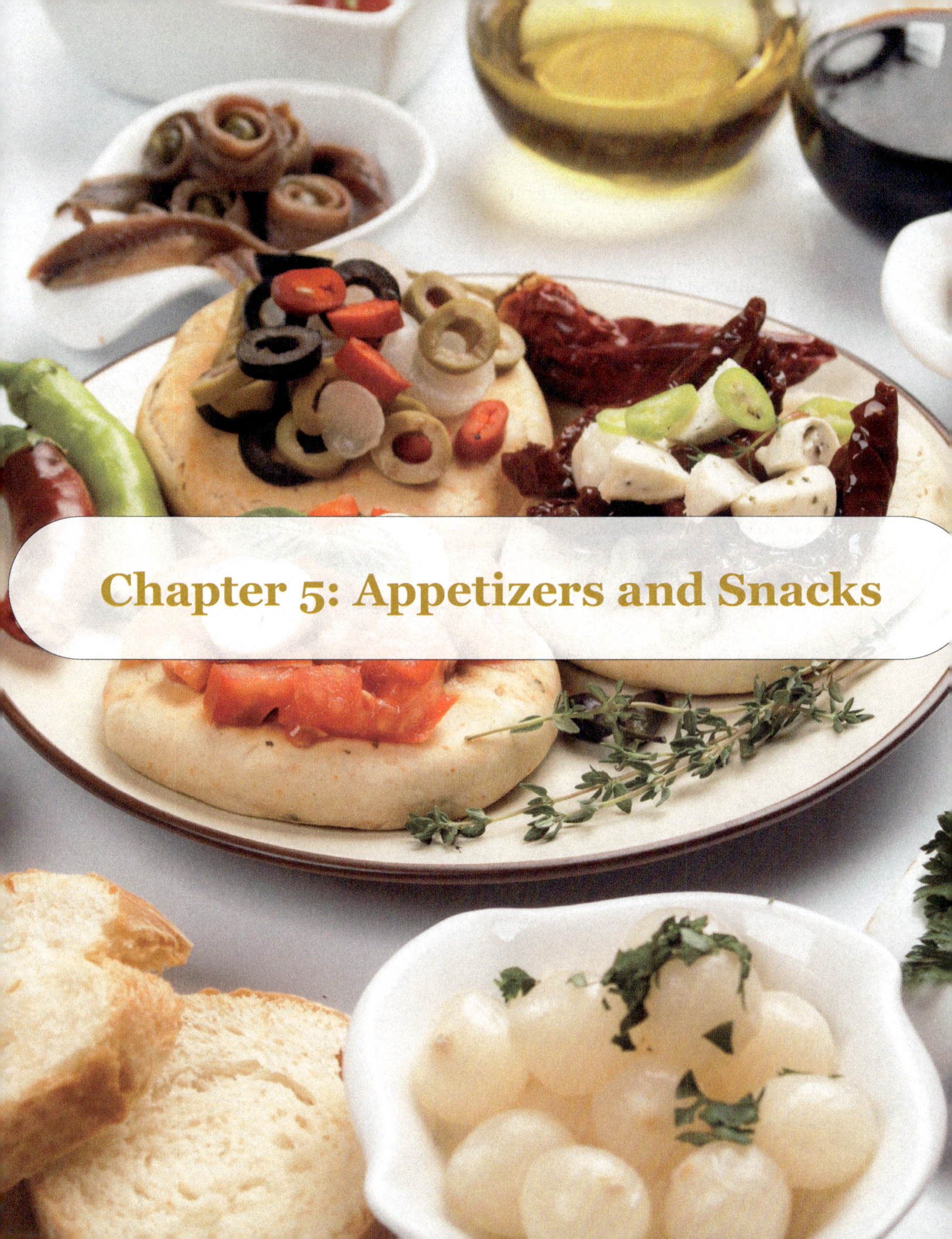

# Chapter 5: Appetizers and Snacks

## Air Fryer Scalloped Potatoes

Prep Time: 10 Mins
Cook Time: 27 Mins      Serves: 4

### Ingredients:

- 6 Medium White Potatoes
- 840 ml Leftover Cheese Sauce
- 50 g Breadcrumbs
- 75 g Grated Cheese
- 1 Tbsp Extra Virgin Olive Oil
- 2 Tsp Chives
- Salt & Pepper

### Directions:

1. Clean the potatoes and then thinly slice and discard the ends.
2. Load the sliced potatoes into a mixing bowl and add the oil and seasonings and mix well with your hands.
3. Load the potatoes into the air fryer basket and air fry for 15 minutes at 180°C, shake the potatoes, air fry for 8 minutes at 160°C, shake and then spray with extra virgin olive oil spray. Air fry for a further 4 minutes at 200°C.
4. Load the sliced potatoes into your air fryer basket adding a single layer, pour over cheese sauce, and then repeat again 3 more times. Then sprinkle the top of the cheese sauce with breadcrumbs followed by grated cheese.
5. Then air fry for 10 minutes at 180°C before serving.

### Nutritional Value (Amount per Serving):

Calories: 1246; Fat: 44.75; Carb: 186.24; Protein: 25.88

## Air Fryer Duck Fat Potatoes

Prep Time: 5 Mins
Cook Time: 10 Mins      Serves: 2

### Ingredients:

- 500 g White Potatoes
- 2 Tbsp Duck Fat
- 1 Tsp Garlic Powder
- 2 Tsp Rosemary
- Salt & Pepper

### Directions:

1. Peel and dice your white potatoes into your preferred size of roast potatoes.
2. Load into a bowl with your seasoning and your duck fat. Toss with your hands until potatoes are well coated.
3. Load into the air fryer basket. Cook for 15 minutes at 160°C.
4. Shake the air fryer basket and check that the potatoes are cooked by placing a potato on a fork. Cook for a further 5 minutes at 200°C.
5. Serve.

**Nutritional Value (Amount per Serving):**

Calories: 363; Fat: 13.27; Carb: 56.2; Protein: 5.87

## Air Fryer Butternut Squash Cubes

Prep Time: 5 Mins
Cook Time: 20 Mins          Serves: 4

### Ingredients:

- 500 g Butternut Squash
- ½ Tbsp Extra Virgin Olive Oil
- 1 Tsp Garlic Powder
- 2 Tsp Thyme
- 2 Tsp Parsley
- Salt & Pepper

### Directions:

1. Peel and slice your butternut squash into butternut squash cubes, making sure you get rid of all the seeds.
2. Remove any fleshy/soft bits of butternut squash.
3. Load your butternut squash into a bowl with the rest of the ingredients and mix well with your hands.
4. Load the butternut squash cubes into the air fryer and cook for 15 minutes at 160°C.
5. Shake the air fryer basket and test with a fork that your butternut squash is cooked.
6. Cook for a further 5 minutes at 180°C to make your butternut squash crispy like roasted butternut squash.
7. Serve.

**Nutritional Value (Amount per Serving):**

Calories: 65; Fat: 0.93; Carb: 14.84; Protein: 1.34

# Air Fryer Butternut Squash Fries

Prep Time: 5 Mins
Cook Time: 14 Mins     Serves: 4

## Ingredients:

- 450 g Butternut Squash
- ½ Tbsp Extra Virgin Olive Oil
- 1 Tsp Garlic Powder
- 2 Tsp Bouquet Garni
- Salt & Pepper

## Directions:

1. Peel and slice your butternut squash into butternut squash fries.
2. Remove any fleshy/soft bits of butternut squash. Slice into fries.
3. Load your butternut squash into a bowl with the rest of the ingredients and mix well with your hands.
4. Load the butternut squash fries into the air fryer and cook for 12 minutes at 160°C.
5. Shake the air fryer basket and test with a fork that your butternut squash fries are cooked.
6. Cook for a further 2 minutes at 180°C to make your butternut squash fries crispy. Serve with your favourite dipping sauce.

## Nutritional Value (Amount per Serving):

Calories: 59; Fat: 0.9; Carb: 13.4; Protein: 1.2

# Air Fryer Frozen Corn Dogs

Prep Time: 1 Min
Cook Time: 12 Mins     Serves: 12

## Ingredients:

- 1 Box Frozen Corn Dogs

## Directions:

1. Remove packaging from corn dogs and load the frozen corn dogs into your air fryer basket.
2. Cook for 12 minutes at 190°C.
3. Serve with your favourite corn dog dipping sauces.

**Nutritional Value (Amount per Serving):**

Calories: 208; Fat: 10.02; Carb: 22.47; Protein: 7.14

## Tyson Popcorn Chicken In Air Fryer

Prep Time: 1 Min
Cook Time: 8 Mins    Serves: 2

### Ingredients:

- 1 Pack Frozen Tyson Popcorn Chicken

### Directions:

1. Remove frozen popcorn chicken from the packaging.
2. Give it a quick shake to remove any loose bits of batter.
3. Place into your air fryer basket making sure that the popcorn chicken is not overcrowded.
4. Cook for 8 minutes at 170°C.
5. Serve with your favourite dipping sauce.

**Nutritional Value (Amount per Serving):**

Calories: 529; Fat: 12.88; Carb: 0; Protein: 96.97

## Air Fryer Chicken Thighs Potatoes

Prep Time: 5 Mins
Cook Time: 25 Mins    Serves: 4

### Ingredients:

- 8 Chicken Thighs
- 6 Medium White Potatoes
- 1 Tsp Extra Virgin Olive Oil
- 2 Tsp Garlic Puree
- 1 Tsp Oregano
- 1 Tbsp Honey
- 2 Tsp Mustard
- Salt & Pepper

### Directions:

1. Slice your potatoes into either chunks or small slices. Load into a bowl and toss in extra virgin olive oil. Season with salt, pepper and oregano.

2. Place the potatoes into your air fryer basket.
3. In a little bowl mix together garlic, mustard and honey.
4. Brush the skin of your chicken thighs with the marinade and season with salt and pepper too. Add a sprinkle of oregano.
5. Load the chicken thighs over the potatoes with skin side up and cook for 180°C for 15 minutes.
6. Shake the basket so that the potatoes don't become stuck to the basket. Turn the chicken thighs over so that skin side is now down.
7. Cook for a further 10 minutes at 160°C.

### Nutritional Value (Amount per Serving):

Calories: 1103; Fat: 65.05; Carb: 57.38; Protein: 69.53

## Air Fryer Pizza Fries

Prep Time: 10 Mins
Cook Time: 18 Mins     Serves: 2

### Ingredients:

- 2 Large Potatoes
- 1 Tbsp Extra Virgin Olive Oil
- 2 Tsp Oregano
- Salt & Pepper
- 150 g Grated Cheese
- 1 Chorizo thinly sliced

### Directions:

1. Peel and slice your potatoes into chips.
   Load the potatoes into a bowl, add seasoning and extra virgin olive oil and toss until nicely coated.
2. Load the fries into the air fryer basket and cook for 15 minutes at 160°C.
3. When it beeps shake the chips and make sure a fork goes through a chip and they are not underdone.
4. Add pizza toppings to the top of the fries while they are still in the air fryer basket.
5. Cook for a further 3 minutes at 200°C or until the cheese is perfectly melted.
6. Serve with your favourite pizza dipping sauce.

### Nutritional Value (Amount per Serving):

Calories: 677; Fat: 30.85; Carb: 74.49; Protein: 27.44

# Slimming World Chicken Kebab In The Air Fryer

Prep Time: 5 Mins
Cook Time: 20 Mins     Serves: 4

## Ingredients:

- 600 g Chicken Breast
- 2 Tsp Extra Virgin Olive Oil
- 1 Tsp Coriander
- 1 Tsp Paprika
- 1 Tsp Oregano
- 1 Tsp Mixed Spice
- Pinch Cayenne Pepper
- 1 Tsp Garlic
- 1 Tsp Onion
- Salt & Pepper

## Directions:

1. Dice your chicken breast and season with salt and pepper.
2. In a ramekin add your dried seasonings and mix well.
3. Load the seasonings into a bowl with the chicken breast and mix well.
4. Place in the fridge for at least 3 hours for the chicken to marinade.
5. Remove the chicken from the fridge, load onto skewers and add a little olive oil over the kebabs.
6. Place the chicken kebabs in the air fryer basket and cook for 10 minutes at 180°C. Turn and cook for a further 10 minutes.
7. Serve.

## Nutritional Value (Amount per Serving):

Calories: 292; Fat: 15.3; Carb: 5.46; Protein: 32.14

# Chapter 6: Wraps and Sandwiches

# Air Fryer Hot Dogs

Prep Time: 5 Mins
Cook Time: 10 Mins     Serves: 6

### Ingredients:

- 6 hot dogs
- 6 hot dog buns

### Directions:

1. Place hot dogs in basket of air fryer. Cook at 200°C for 4 minutes. Remove from basket.
2. Place buns in basket and cook at 200°C for 2 minutes to toast them, if desired.
3. Place hot dogs in buns and top with desired toppings.

### Nutritional Value (Amount per Serving):

Calories: 345; Fat: 18.4; Carb: 26.15; Protein: 17.87

# Air Fryer Frozen Burritos

Prep Time: 1 Min
Cook Time: 6 Mins     Serves: 4

### Ingredients:

- Frozen Burritos

### Directions:

1. Remove the frozen burritos from the packaging and place into the air fryer basket on a bed of foil.
2. Air fry frozen burrito for 6 minutes at 180°C before serving.
3. For large frozen burritos place in the air fryer basket (no need for foil) and air fry for 18 minutes at 160°C to defrost in the middle.
4. Then finish with a further 17 minutes at 180°C before serving.

### Nutritional Value (Amount per Serving):

Calories: 318; Fat: 9; Carb: 54; Protein: 7.5

# Air Fryer Ham Cheese Sandwich

Prep Time: 2 Mins
Cook Time: 6 Mins      Serves: 4

### Ingredients:

- 8 Slices Bread
- 8 Slices Cheese
- 200 g Ham
- Butter

### Directions:

1. Butter a slice of bread.
2. Add a slice of cheese, ham, then another slice of cheese.
3. Place a cocktail stick in the top of the cheese to secure it.
4. Load into the air fryer and cook for 3 minutes at 200°C.
5. Remove the cocktail stick.
6. Add a slice a bread, add butter on top and air fry for a further 3 minutes at 200°C.
7. Serve.

### Nutritional Value (Amount per Serving):

Calories: 372; Fat: 19.4; Carb: 26.19; Protein: 23.26

# Air Fryer Yorkshire Pudding Wrap

Prep Time: 2 Mins
Cook Time: 4 Mins      Serves: 2

### Ingredients:

- 400 g Leftover Roast Dinner
- 2 Giant Yorkshire Puddings frozen

### Directions:

1. Place your frozen Yorkshire pudding in the air fryer and cook for 1 minute at 180°C.
2. Flatten the Yorkshire pudding with either your hand or a rolling pin.
3. Load the Yorkshire pudding with a mix of your leftovers and then place the loaded Yorkshire pudding back in the air fryer.
4. Air fry for a further 3 minutes at 180°C or until piping hot. Fold your

Yorkshire pudding in half to transform into a wrap before tucking in.

**Nutritional Value (Amount per Serving):**

Calories: 426; Fat: 27; Carb: 13.8; Protein: 32

## Air Fryer Bacon Wrapped Scallops

Prep Time: 5 Mins
Cook Time: 8 Mins    Serves: 2

### Ingredients:

- 1 Bag Frozen Scallops thawed
- 1 Pack Back Bacon
- Salt & Pepper

### Directions:

1. Thaw your scallops and then pat dry with kitchen towel.
2. Slice your back bacon lengthways so each bacon slice becomes two long slices.
3. Season your scallops with salt and pepper.
4. Wrap each scallop in bacon and then secure in place with a cocktail stick. Place into the air fryer.
5. Air fry for 8 minutes at 180°C before serving.

**Nutritional Value (Amount per Serving):**

Calories: 35; Fat: 1.32; Carb: 5.46; Protein: 1.03

## Air Fryer Part Baked Bread Rolls

Prep Time: 2 Mins
Cook Time: 14 Mins    Serves: 4

### Ingredients:

- 6 Pack Part Baked Bread Rolls
- Extra Virgin Olive Oil Spray
- 1 Tbsp Butter
- 10 Thick Sausages optional
- Mayonnaise optional

### Directions:

1. Place your sausages into the air fryer basket and cook for 8 minutes at 180°C, or a little longer if not fully cooked.

2. Now that your sausages are cooked (they will be golden thanks to the air fryer) remove the sausages and allow them to cool a little on a plate.
3. Place your part baked rolls into the air fryer basket, spray with extra virgin olive oil and air fry for 6 minutes at 180°C.
4. When the air fryer beeps, they will be golden and crispy.
5. Load them onto a plate and then butter the rolls and load them up with sausages and mayonnaise.

### Nutritional Value (Amount per Serving):

Calories: 707; Fat: 27.76; Carb: 88.98; Protein: 28.97

## Air Fryer S'Mores

Prep Time: 2 Mins
Cook Time: 6 Mins    Serves: 4

### Ingredients:

- 8 Graham Crackers
- 4 Marshmallows
- 8 Squares Galaxy Chocolate

### Directions:

1. Gather your ingredients and make sure you have a marshmallow for each air fried smore as well as 2 squares of chocolate for each. Also make sure your chocolate is at room temperature.
2. Slice in half the marshmallows width not length so that they will be sticky.
3. Then place the two sticky halves of the marshmallow onto the crackers and load into the air fryer basket.
4. Air fry for 6 minutes at 180°C for until the marshmallow is golden on top like it is when you grill it.
5. Then before the marshmallow cools, place the chocolate on top of each marshmallow half and then place the cracker on top.
6. Serve once the chocolate has melted onto the marshmallow.

### Nutritional Value (Amount per Serving):

Calories: 458; Fat: 33.49; Carb: 30.91; Protein: 9.07

# Air Fryer Halloumi Gyros

Prep Time: 5 Mins
Cook Time: 7 Mins     Serves: 6

### Ingredients:

- 225 g Halloumi
- 50 g Leftover Air Fryer Chips
- 6 WW Wraps
- 10 g Sliced Cumber
- 10 g Halved Cherry Tomatoes
- reek Dip
- 1 Tbsp Chopped Fresh Mint
- 1 tsp Lemon Juice 1/4 Lemon
- 10 g Cucumber Sliced 1/4 Medium Cucumber
- 1 Tsp Garlic Puree
- 6 Tbsp Greek Yoghurt

### Directions:

1. Slice your halloumi into 6 portions and place in the air fryer. Air fry for 5 minutes at 180°C.
2. When the air fryer beeps add the chips to one side and cook for a further 2 minutes on the same temperature.
3. When the air fryer is cooking the halloumi add all the dip ingredients into a bowl and mix well.
4. When the air fryer beeps add a slice of halloumi, some chips, sliced cucumber and tomato and dip to a wrap and serve. Rinse and repeat for all 6 wraps.

### Nutritional Value (Amount per Serving):

Calories: 638; Fat: 31.13; Carb: 38.03; Protein: 50.51

# My Air fry 2 Cheese Tomato Toastie

Prep Time: 2 Mins
Cook Time: 8 Mins     Serves: 1

## Ingredients:

- 6 thin Slices Chedder Cheese
- 2 Slices Halloumi
- 3 Cherry Tomatoes smashed and mashed
- 1 little pinch of ground Black pepper
- Butter for the outsides of the bread or a tasty oil spray

## Directions:

1. Lay half the slices of the chedder cheese on the unbuttoned side of the bread
2. Add the Slice of Halloumi then add the mashed Tomatoes on top of the halloumi add the pepper on top.
3. Add the other slice of cheeder cheese on top of tomatoes
4. Add the top slice on top and add on parchment paper cut to fit the the try in the airfry then add 2 toothpicks right through to hold the sandwich in place.
5. Air-fry at 200 °C for about 5 minutes then turn over for a further 3- 4 minutes (a good 5 minutes each side for Wholemeal Bread) for the cheese to melt and Wholemeal Bread to brown. Serve and Enjoy

## Nutritional Value (Amount per Serving):

Calories: 1245; Fat: 107.57; Carb: 9.44; Protein: 61.58

# Chapter 7: Casseroles, Frittatas, and Quiches

## Air Fryer Cheese Quiche

Prep Time: 15 Mins
Cook Time: 18 Mins    Serves: 2

### Ingredients:

- 300 g Air Fryer Pie Crust
- 300 g Grated Cheddar Cheese
- 4 Cherry Tomatoes
- 75 ml Whole Milk
- 3 Large Eggs
- 1 Tbsp Oregano
- 2 Tsp Mixed Herbs
- Salt & Pepper

### Directions:

1. Start by making your pie crust. Add mixed herbs into the crust to give it a better flavour. Roll out into ramekins or other similar containers.
2. Using a mixing jug beat eggs with milk and add in salt and pepper.
3. Add grated cheese into your ramekins until ¾ full and then pour over your milk and egg mixture to just over ¾ full. Slice in half cherry tomatoes and load over the mixture, then add a sprinkle of extra grated cheese and oregano.
4. Air fry for 8 minutes at 180°C followed by a further 10 minutes at 160°C.

### Nutritional Value (Amount per Serving):

Calories: 1152; Fat: 66.94; Carb: 102.62; Protein: 35.91

## Easter Egg Cookies

Prep Time: 10 Mins
Cook Time: 15 Mins    Serves: 20

### Ingredients:

- 110g Unsalted Butter, at room temperature
- 100g Light Brown Sugar
- 75g Caster Sugar
- 2 Eggs
- 1 tsp Vanilla extract
- 185g Plain Flour
- 1/2 tsp Salt

- 1/2 tsp Bicarbonate of Soda
- 1/2 tsp Baking Powder
- 80g Mini Eggs, bashed to sort uneven pieces

### Directions:

1. Add Butter, Light Brown Sugar, Caster Sugar to a large bowl and beat till creamy.
2. Beat in the Eggs and Vanilla.
3. Sieve in the Flour, Salt, Bicarbonate of Soda. Fold in with a wooden spoon.
4. Stir in the Mini Eggs.
5. Use a teaspoon to portion the dough into 20 – 25 scoops, then press each cookie down to flatten.
6. Once the unit has preheated, bake the cookies on greaseproof paper, in batches (with 1 inch space between each cookie) at 160°C for 8 minutes using the Bake function. I do 5 at a time.
7. Leave to set for 5 minutes.
8. Allow to cool for 10 minutes.

### Nutritional Value (Amount per Serving):

Calories: 110; Fat: 5.03; Carb: 13.24; Protein: 2.73

## Cheesy Masala Omelette Quesadilla

Prep Time: 5 Mins
Cook Time: 5 Mins          Serves: 2

### Ingredients:

- 4 Eggs
- 1/2 Onion finely diced
- 1 clove of Garlic sliced finely
- 1 - 2 Green Chillies finely chopped, adjust quantity to taste
- Small Handful Fresh Coriander finely chopped
- 1/4 tsp Ground Coriander Optional
- 1/4 tsp Ground Cumin Optional
- 1/4 tsp Ground Turmeric
- 1/2 tsp Red Chilli Powder
- 1/2 tsp Salt Or to taste
- 1/2 tsp Black Pepper Optional
- 2 tbsp Milk, Optional
- 2 tbsp Ghee or Butter
- 4 tbsp Cheddar, grated

- 4 Tortillas

**Directions:**

1. In a bowl, beat the eggs, then add all the other ingredients minus the ghee
2. In a wide, nonstick frying pan, heat the ghee or butter over a medium heat.
3. Add half the egg mixture to the pan and leave to set, before flipping to cook the other side.
4. Transfer the omelette from the pan on to a plate and keep warm. Repeat for the second omelette.
5. Preheat the Air Fryer.
6. Add Tortilla to the Foodi.
7. Add omelette and sprinkle over Cheese.
8. Top with another Tortilla.
9. Weigh down with a metal trivet or secure with toothpicks.
10. Air Fry at 180°C for 5 minutes.

**Nutritional Value (Amount per Serving):**

Calories: 924; Fat: 54.47; Carb: 65.33; Protein: 42.96

## Air Fryer Cheese Flan

Prep Time: 10 Mins
Cook Time: 17 Mins     Serves: 8

**Ingredients:**

- Air Fryer Pie Crust
- ½ Small Onion diced
- 4 Large Eggs
- 120 ml Semi Skimmed Milk
- 180 g Grated Cheese
- 2 Tsp Parsley
- Salt & Pepper

**Directions:**

1. Make your shortcrust pastry and then roll it out and add it to your tart tin.
2. Fork the bottom of the pastry to let it breathe.
3. Then add sliced onion to the bottom of the flan.
4. Mix with a fork your eggs, milk and seasoning.
5. Add the cheese and mix well.
6. Pour the cheese and egg mixture over the onions and then place the cheese flan into the air fryer.
7. Cook your cheese flan for 17 minutes at 160°C or until a cocktail stick comes out clean.

8. Then slice into squares like school dinner flan.

**Nutritional Value (Amount per Serving):**

Calories: 218; Fat: 14.32; Carb: 14.11; Protein: 8.23

## Air Fryer Tortilla De Patatas (Spanish Omelette)

Prep Time: 6 Mins
Cook Time: 44 Mins          Serves: 8

**Ingredients:**

- 500 g Baby Potatoes
- 6 Large Eggs
- 2 Tsp Extra Virgin Olive Oil
- Extra Virgin Olive Oil Spray
- Sea Salt

**Directions:**

1. Chop your baby potatoes into medium slices, keeping the skin on them. Load the potatoes into a bowl and toss in extra virgin olive oil and salt.
2. Load the potatoes into the air fryer basket and cook for 17 minutes at 180°C.
3. In a jug add your eggs, a little sea seal and mix with a fork.
4. When the air fryer beeps, load potatoes into a silicone baking pan and pour over the egg mixture. And make sure all the potatoes are well covered in the egg batter.
5. Place the silicone pan into the air fryer basket and cook for 17 minutes at 160°C, followed by 5 minutes at 180°C to ensure its cooked in the middle and the eggs have set.
6. Turn the potato omelette over, spray with extra virgin olive oil and cook for a further 5 minutes at 180°C.
7. Then slice your Spanish omelette and serve.

**Nutritional Value (Amount per Serving):**

Calories: 109; Fat: 5.63; Carb: 11.38; Protein: 3.29

# Air Fryer Frozen Falafel Bowl

Prep Time: 5 Mins
Cook Time: 18 Mins        Serves: 2

## Ingredients:

- 15 Frozen Falafel Balls
- ½ Yellow Pepper
- ½ Red Pepper
- ½ Medium Courgette
- ½ Can Drained Chickpeas
- 2 Tsp Cumin
- 2 Tsp Coriander
- Sliced Tomatoes
- Greek Dip
- 6 Tbsp Greek Yoghurt heaped
- 1 Tbsp Fresh Mint shredded
- ¼ Cucumber small chunks
- ¼ Tsp Garlic Puree
- 2 Tsp Lemon Juice
- 1 Tsp Dill

## Directions:

1. Slice and dice your veggies and toss them in half the coriander and cumin. Also season them with salt and pepper.
2. Load the veggies into the air fryer with the frozen falafels and cook for 8 minutes at 180°C. Shake and then air fry for a further 3 minutes at the same temperature.
3. Once cooked remove from the air fryer and load into a bowl.
4. Season drained chickpeas in the rest of the cumin and coriander and season with salt and pepper. Air fry for 6 minutes at 180°C. Whilst the chickpeas are being air fried load into a bowl your Greek dip ingredients and mix well. Load the dip and sliced tomatoes onto your falafel bowl.
5. Then when the air fryer beeps, add the chickpeas, and serve with the rest of your falafel bowl.

## Nutritional Value (Amount per Serving):

Calories: 181; Fat: 3.46; Carb: 24.06; Protein: 15.42

# Air Fryer Frittata

Prep Time: 10 Mins
Cook Time: 39 Mins          Serves: 8

## Ingredients:

- 8 Large Eggs
- 240 ml Mascarpone
- 200 g Grated Reduced Fat Cheddar
- 6 Reduced Fat Sausages sliced into quarters
- 1 Large Sweet Potato
- 1 Medium Zucchini/Courgette
- 1 Tbsp Extra Virgin Olive Oil
- 2 Spring Onions sliced
- 1 Tsp Parsley
- Salt & Pepper
- Sliced Cherry Tomatoes optional
- Sprinkle Basil optional

## Directions:

1. Peel and dice your sweet potato into cubes. Slice your zucchini into medium slices and then quarter each slice. Load into a bowl the zucchini and sweet potato with a tablespoon of extra virgin olive oil, salt, pepper, and parsley. Mix with your hands.
2. Load the sweet potato and zucchini into the air fryer basket and air fry for 5 minutes at 180°C.
3. Shake the air fryer and add the sausages on top and air fry for a further 12 minutes.
4. Load the filling items (zucchini and sweet potato) as well as some spring onion we sliced into the silicone dishes.
5. In a measuring jug add eggs and beat with a fork and then slowly add in the cream. Season with salt, pepper, and parsley.
6. Add grated cheese to the silicone and then pour over the egg and cream mixture. Decorate with cherry tomato halves as well as a sprinkle of basil.
7. Place the silicone in the air fryer and air fry for 17 minutes at 180°C followed by a further 5 minutes at 170°C. Check with a cocktail stick in the centre and if it comes out clean then the frittata is cooked.
8. Once its cool enough to touch, peel the silicone from the frittata.
9. Then slice into quarters and place in the fridge ready for breakfast for the next few days.

## Nutritional Value (Amount per Serving):

Calories: 440; Fat: 36.43; Carb: 22.6; Protein: 8.02

# Chapter 8: Desserts

## Air Fryer Frozen Eclairs

Prep Time: 1 Min
Cook Time: 6 Mins    Serves: 2

### Ingredients:

- 1 Box Frozen Mini Chocolate Eclairs

### Directions:

1. Remove the frozen chocolate eclairs from the packaging and place into the air fryer basket.
2. Air fry for 4 minutes at 160°C and then turn the temperature down to 140c and cook for a further 2 minutes before serving.

### Nutritional Value (Amount per Serving):

Calories: 15; Fat: 0.11; Carb: 2.8; Protein: 0.62

## Air Fryer Frozen Portuguese Egg Tarts

Prep Time: 1 Min
Cook Time: 9 Mins    Serves: 4

### Ingredients:

- 4 Frozen Portuguese Egg Custard Tarts

### Directions:

1. Remove frozen Portuguese tarts from the packaging but keeping the foil container and place in the air fryer.
2. Make sure the egg tarts are spread out and not on top of one another.
3. Air fry for 9 minutes at 160°C before serving.

### Nutritional Value (Amount per Serving):

Calories: 349; Fat: 5.44; Carb: 70.38; Protein: 5.87

# Three Ingredient Air fryer Apple Chips

Prep Time: 2 Mins
Cook Time: 10 Mins     Serves: 1

### Ingredients:

- 6 Large Red Apples
- 1Tsp Olive Oil
- 1 Pinch Cinnamon

### Directions:

1. Slide up your apple into nice bite sized chunks.
2. Place them in the air fryer and drizzle with a teaspoon of olive oil.
3. Cook on a 180°C for 10 minutes or until nice and crisp.
4. Toss them in cinnamon in a large bowl.
5. Serve!

### Nutritional Value (Amount per Serving):

Calories: 967; Fat: 7.65; Carb: 221.43; Protein: 4.32

# Air Fry Banana In Syrup And Nutella

Prep Time: 2 Mins
Cook Time: 10 Mins     Serves: 1

### Ingredients:

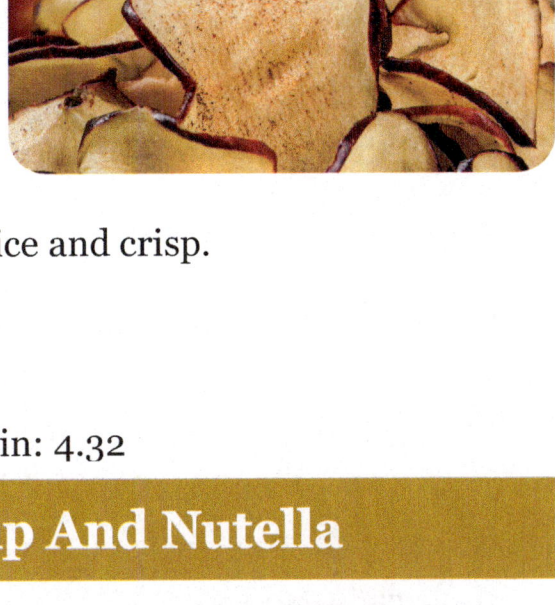

- 2-3 banana, sliced (use up ripped)
- Toppings
- Maple Syrup
- Nutella
- Butter (optional)

### Directions:

1. Place banana in the air fryer. Set it for 180°C for 10 min. Open to turn over half way.
2. Once cooked in air fryer, plate up and too with maple syrup, honey or Nutella or on its own with a little bit of butter

### Nutritional Value (Amount per Serving):

Calories: 1520; Fat: 33.11; Carb: 317.04; Protein: 14.47

# Three Ingredient Air fryer Shortbread Fingers

Prep Time: 4 Mins
Cook Time: 12 Mins    Serves: 10

### Ingredients:

- 175g Butter
- 75g Caster Sugar
- 250g Plain Flour

### Directions:

1. Preheat your airfryer to 180°C.
2. Mix flour and sugar in a bowl.
3. Add the butter and rub into the flour and sugar.
4. Knead the mixture well until it is lovely and smooth.
5. Make into finger shapes and decorate with fork markings.
6. Cook in the air fryer on a baking sheet for 12 minutes.

### Nutritional Value (Amount per Serving):

Calories: 187; Fat: 9.91; Carb: 20.85; Protein: 3.31

# Air Fryer Banana Souffle

Prep Time: 3 Mins
Cook Time: 15 Mins    Serves: 4

### Ingredients:

- 2 Medium Bananas
- 2 Large Eggs
- ½ Tsp Cinnamon
- Extra Virgin Olive Oil Spray

### Directions:

1. Peel and the bananas and crack the eggs into the blender. Add your cinnamon and blend on the pulse until smooth.
2. Spray your ramekins with extra virgin olive oil.
3. Pour the souffle batter into the ramekins and place the ramekins in the air fryer basket.
4. Air fry for 15 minutes at 180°C.
5. Serve quickly before the souffles start to fall.

**Nutritional Value (Amount per Serving):**

Calories: 823; Fat: 7.49; Carb: 200.79; Protein: 10.18

## The Ultimate Air fryer Pumpkin Parcels

Prep Time: 5 Mins
Cook Time: 10 Mins      Serves: 9

### Ingredients:

- 3Tbsp Pumpkin Filling
- 1 Sheet Puff Pastry
- 1 Small Egg (beaten)

### Directions:

1. Preheat your air fryer to 180°C.
2. Roll out a sheet of puff pastry and layer it with pumpkin pie filling making sure there is a 1cm gap around the edges.
3. Cut it up into 9 square pieces.
4. Cover the gaps with beaten egg so that you will have that lovely egg glow.
5. Place in the air fryer on a baking sheet for 12 minutes at 180°C.
6. Serve!

**Nutritional Value (Amount per Serving):**

Calories: 49; Fat: 3.6; Carb: 2.75; Protein: 1.64

## Healthier Peanut Butter Cookies With Air Fryer

Prep Time: 10 Mins
Cook Time: 20 Mins      Serves: 15

### Ingredients:

- 70 g unsweetened peanut butter
- 30 g almond flour
- ~1 g vanilla extract
- 15 g maple syrup/ honey

### Directions:

1. Mix wet ingredients all together in a bowl
2. Add almond flour into wet mixtures
3. Leave to cool in the fridge for 5-10 mins (i find this helps me to roll the dough into balls)
4. Make 15 small dough balls and flatten them with fork

5. Bake in air fryer 170°C for 15 mins. Then flip side for another 5 mins.

**Nutritional Value (Amount per Serving):**

Calories: 26; Fat: 1.75; Carb: 2.14; Protein: 0.72

## Air Fried Cinnamon Puffs

Prep Time: 4 Mins
Cook Time: 6 Mins        Serves: 2

**Ingredients:**

- Ready rolled puff pastry
- 1 egg, beaten (to egg wash pastry)
- Caster sugar to dust (sweetener for healthier option)
- Grounded cinnamon to dust the pastry

**Directions:**

1. Preheat air frier to 170°C.
2. Cut the pastry into small squares, about 2cm wide.
3. Brush the puff pastry on both sides with the beaten egg.
4. Air fry for 4-6 minutes. While waiting mix cinnamon and sugar together ready for when the pastry comes out of the air fryer.
5. Transfer to a plate and dust both sides with the cinnamon and sugar mix.

**Nutritional Value (Amount per Serving):**

Calories: 226; Fat: 13.79; Carb: 19.37; Protein: 6.25

## Air Fryer Apple Crisp

Prep Time: 15 Mins
Cook Time: 13 Mins        Serves: 4

**Ingredients:**

- 6 Medium Apples
- 1 Tbsp Caster Sugar
- 1 Tbsp Cinnamon
- 120 g Plain Flour
- 40 g Caster Sugar
- 50 g Butter
- 60 g Quick Cook Oats

**Directions:**

1. Peel and dice apples and load into a mixing bowl. Toss in caster sugar and cinnamon. Transfer into ramekins.
2. Load flour and butter into a bowl and rub the fat into the flour until it resembles coarse breadcrumbs. Add sugar and oats until it is well mixed.
3. Add topping onto apples and load the ramekins into the air fryer basket.
4. Start with 160°C for 8 minutes, followed by 200°C for 5 minutes and serve.

**Nutritional Value (Amount per Serving):**

Calories: 348; Fat: 7.83; Carb: 69.39; Protein: 4.99

# CONCLUSION

I wholeheartedly advise anyone who wishes to diversify their air frying techniques to get the Ninja Foodi Dual Zone Air Fryer. The Dual Zone is a true game-changer and streamlines life so much more. Even though the appliance is large, I would find a room for it in my little kitchen. Although it is heavy, the ease of being able to prepare an entire meal at once more than makes up for this. My microwave and oven felt quite neglected as a result.

# APPENDIX RECIPE INDEX

**A**

Air Fryer Toasted Bagels ................. 18
Air Fryer Quesadilla ..................... 18
Air Fryer Soft Boiled Eggs ............... 20
Air Fryer Crumpets ....................... 20
Air Fried Beef Sausage Rolls ............. 21
Air-Fried Eggs ........................... 21
Air Fried Bacon And Poached Eggs ......... 22
Air Fryer Baked Smores ................... 23
Air Fryer Frozen Breaded Mushrooms ....... 25
Air Fryer Kohlrabi Fries ................. 26
Air Fryer Corn On The Cob ................ 26
Air Fryer Radishes ....................... 27
Air Fryer Cabbage ........................ 27
Air Fryer Asparagus ...................... 28
Air-Fried Onion With Balsamic Vinegar .... 30
Air Fryer Pork Loin ...................... 32
Air Fried Fish With Sweet Chilli Leafs ... 33
Air Fryer Sausages ....................... 34
Air Fryer Meatballs ...................... 34
Air Fryer Pork Chops ..................... 35
Air Fryer Bacon .......................... 35
Air Fryer Steak Bites .................... 36
Air Fryer Frozen Sausages ................ 37
Air-Fried Chicken ........................ 39
Air Fryer Tgi Friday Boneless Chicken Wings ... 41
Air Fryer Chicken Wrapped In Bacon ....... 42
Air Fryer Piri Piri Chicken Legs ......... 42
Air Fryer Scalloped Potatoes ............. 45
Air Fryer Duck Fat Potatoes .............. 45
Air Fryer Butternut Squash Cubes ......... 46
Air Fryer Butternut Squash Fries ......... 47
Air Fryer Frozen Corn Dogs ............... 47
Air Fryer Chicken Thighs Potatoes ........ 48
Air Fryer Pizza Fries .................... 49
Air Fryer Hot Dogs ....................... 52
Air Fryer Frozen Burritos ................ 52
Air Fryer Ham Cheese Sandwich ............ 53
Air Fryer Yorkshire Pudding Wrap ......... 53
Air Fryer Bacon Wrapped Scallops ......... 54
Air Fryer Part Baked Bread Rolls ......... 54
Air Fryer S'Mores ........................ 55
Air Fryer Halloumi Gyros ................. 56
Air Fryer Cheese Quiche .................. 59
Air Fryer Cheese Flan .................... 61
Air Fryer Tortilla De Patatas (Spanish Omelette) .. 62

Air Fryer Frozen Falafel Bowl ............ 63
Air Fryer Frittata ....................... 64
Air Fryer Frozen Eclairs ................. 66
Air Fryer Frozen Portuguese Egg Tarts .... 66
Air Fry Banana In Syrup And Nutella ...... 67
Air Fryer Banana Souffle ................. 68
Air Fried Cinnamon Puffs ................. 70
Air Fryer Apple Crisp .................... 70

**C**

Cajun Air-Fried Potatoes ................. 28
Crispy Air Fryer Bacon ................... 36
Chicken Wings, Drumsticks And Thighs In Air Fryer ... 40
Cheesy Masala Omelette Quesadilla ........ 60

**E**

Easter Egg Cookies ....................... 59

**H**

Hot Juicy Air Fried Chicken Wings ........ 43
Healthier Peanut Butter Cookies With Air Fryer 69

**L**

My Crisp Bacon Cheese Wrapped Breast With Asparagus ... 19

**M**

My Salt Rainbow Peppered Buttered Asparagus 29
My Air fryer Crispy Ham And Cheese Rolls ... 33
10-Minute Chicken Pizza .................. 39
My Air fry 2 Cheese Tomato Toastie ....... 57

**P**

Padron Peppers ........................... 25

**R**

Rosemary Roast Potatoes Air Fryer Style .. 29
Reheat Fried Chicken In Air Fryer ........ 40

**T**

Tyson Chicken Wings In Air Fryer ......... 41
Tyson Popcorn Chicken In Air Fryer ....... 48
Three Ingredient Air fryer Apple Chips ... 67
Three Ingredient Air fryer Shortbread Fingers . 68
The Ultimate Air fryer Pumpkin Parcels ... 69

**S**

Spanish Seasoned Pork Loin Steaks ........ 32
Slimming World Chicken Kebab In The Air Fryer 50

Printed in Great Britain
by Amazon